J. S. Bach Mandolin Duets

by John Holenko

© 2017 by Mel Bay Publications, Inc. All Rights Reserved.

WWW.MELBAY.COM

John Holenko

John Holenko has performed on classical guitar, steel-string guitar, mandolin, banjo and historic instruments throughout the United States and in Europe. Called "a skilled soloist" by The Boston Globe, he has given recitals and been featured in radio broadcasts throughout the U.S. As a member of the of the early music ensemble Sonus, he has performed on historic instruments in recitals in the United States and in Europe. He performs on mandolin and steel-string guitar with his group The Hungry Monks, an eclectic, acoustic ensemble playing a wide variety of traditional and original music.

Mr. Holenko lives in Charleston, SC where he has been on the faculty of Charleston Southern University and The College of Charleston. He is also the guitarist, mandolinist, and banjo player for the Charleston Symphony Orchestra. Mr. Holenko is very active in music education through his own private studio, Hungry Monk Music, and residencies through the South Carolina Arts Commission.

Holenko has been an instructor of music at the Charlotte Children's Theatre in Charlotte, NC, the Cuyahoga Valley Environmental Education Center in Ohio, where he has also been Artist-in-Residence, The Green River Preserve in North Carolina, and American Music Systems Summer Workshops. Mel Bay Publications has published his *Renaissance Solos for Mandolin* and *Renaissance Tunebook*. John Holenko received degrees in Classical Guitar Performance from the New England Conservatory, and the University of Southern California, also studying historic performance at both institutions, and premiering many new works.

Preface

These arrangements of Bach's music range from intermediate to advanced. They are mostly dance movements from various keyboard suites, as well as some two-part inventions and a couple of solo pieces arranged for two. In all cases, I have kept the music pretty much intact, with one mandolin playing the right hand of the piano, or the melody, and the other mandolin playing the left hand, or the accompaniment. Octaves have been changed at times to accommodate the range of the mandolin. The "tune" is usually in the 1st mandolin part, but as always with Bach, both parts are interesting and melodic, and contribute to the overall counterpoint.

While I arranged these pieces so that they fit on the mandolin, they could be played as guitar and mandolin duets, with the guitar playing the second part, or even by two guitars.

The tradition of arranging and transcribing Bach's music goes back at least as far as Leopold Stokowski's famous arrangement of the "Toccata in D minor". Nearly every pianist and classical guitarist plays some of Bach's music, even though he didn't actually write for those specific instruments. Bach's music is so strong and well constructed that it seems to transcend specific instrumentation, and while purists may not approve of arrangements of his music, students and professionals can learn a great deal about music by experiencing this music first hand.

Metronome markings are simply suggestions. I have not indicated any ornaments. If you have a sense of Baroque ornamentation, please feel free to add ornaments at will.

I hope you enjoy playing the duet arrangements in this book.

John Holenko

Contents

Aria *Enlightening Thoughts of a Tobacco Smoker* 5
Air from *Partita VI* 6
Andante from *Sonata No. 2 for Solo Violin* 8
Bourrée from *Suite for Lute in E minor* 10
Bourrée from *English Suite No. 2* 11
Bourrée from *French Suite No. 6* 14
Canone IV 16
Courante from *Partita No. 5* 20
Fugue in E minor from *The Well-Tempered Clavier* 22
Gavotte from *English Suite No. 6* 25
Gavotte I from *Suite for Lute, BWV 995* 26
Gavotte II from *Suite for Lute, BWV 995* 28
Gigue from *English Suite No. 2* 30
Gigue from *French Suite No. 6* 33
Invention No. 1 36
Invention No. 4 38
Invention No. 10 40
Little Prelude No. 6 from *6 Little Preludes* 42
March from *The Anna Magdalena Notebook* 44
Menuet in A minor from *The Anna Magdalena Notebook* 45
Menuet from *French Suite No. 3* 46
Menuet from *French Suite No. 4* 48
Menuet in D minor from *The Anna Magdalena Notebook* 49
Menuet in G from *The Anna Magdalena Notebook* 50
Menuet in G minor from *The Anna Magdalena Notebook* 51
Menuet in G from *The Anna Magdalena Notebook* 52
Musette from *The Anna Magdalena Notebook* 54
Musette 55
Prelude No. 5 from *The Well-Tempered Clavier* 56
Prelude in D minor 60
Prelude in F from *the Little Clavier Book for W. F. Bach* 62
Preludio 64
Rondeau from *Partita No. 2* 66
Sarabande from *Partita No. 2* 70
Polonaise from *The Anna Magdalena Notebook* 72

Aria
Enlightening Thoughts of a Tobacco Smoker

J. S. Bach
*arranged for 2 mandolins
by John Holenko*

Air
from *Partita VI*

J. S. Bach
*arranged for 2 mandolins
by John Holenko*

Andante
from *Sonata No. 2 for Solo Violin*

J. S. Bach
*arranged for 2 mandolins
by John Holenko*

8

Bourrée
from *Suite for Lute in E minor*

J. S. Bach
*arranged for 2 mandolins
by John Holenko*

10

Bourrée
from *English Suite No. 2*

J. S. Bach
*arranged for 2 mandolins
by John Holenko*

11

Bourrée
from *French Suite No. 6*

J. S. Bach
*arranged for 2 mandolins
by John Holenko*

Canone IV

J. S. Bach
*arranged for 2 mandolins
by John Holenko*

Courante
from *Partita No. 5*

J. S. Bach
*arranged for 2 mandolins
by John Holenko*

Fugue in E minor
from *The Well-Tempered Clavier*

J. S. Bach
*arranged for 2 mandolins
by John Holenko*

Gavotte
from *English Suite No. 6*

J. S. Bach
*arranged for 2 mandolins
by John Holenko*

25

Gavotte I
from *Suite for Lute,* BWV 995

J. S. Bach
*arranged for 2 mandolins
by John Holenko*

Gavotte II
from *Suite for Lute,* BWV 995

J. S. Bach
*arranged for 2 mandolins
by John Holenko*

Gigue
from *English Suite No. 2*

J. S. Bach
*arranged for 2 mandolins
by John Holenko*

30

Gigue
from *French Suite No. 6*

J. S. Bach
arranged for 2 mandolins
by John Holenko

35

Invention No. 1

J. S. Bach
*arranged for 2 mandolins
by John Holenko*

Invention No. 4

J. S. Bach
*arranged for 2 mandolins
by John Holenko*

Invention No. 10

J. S. Bach
*arranged for 2 mandolins
by John Holenko*

40

Little Prelude No. 6
from *6 Little Preludes*

J. S. Bach
*arranged for 2 mandolins
by John Holenko*

March
from *The Anna Magdalena Notebook*

J. S. Bach
arranged for 2 mandolins
by John Holenko

Menuet in A minor
from *The Anna Magdalena Notebook*

J. S. Bach
*arranged for 2 mandolins
by John Holenko*

Menuet
from *French Suite No. 3*

J. S. Bach
arranged for 2 mandolins
by John Holenko

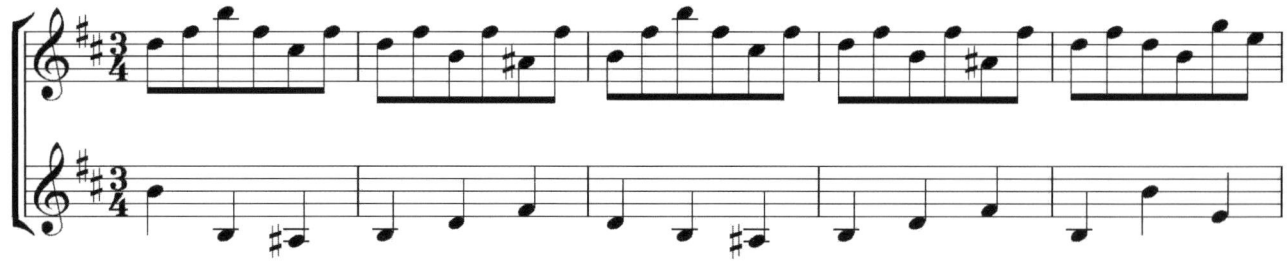

Menuet
from *French Suite No. 4*

J. S. Bach
*arranged for 2 mandolins
by John Holenko*

48

Menuet in D minor
from *The Anna Magdalena Notebook*

J. S. Bach
*arranged for 2 mandolins
by John Holenko*

Menuet in G
from *The Anna Magdalena Notebook*

J. S. Bach
*arranged for 2 mandolins
by John Holenko*

50

Menuet in G minor
from *The Anna Magdalena Notebook*

J. S. Bach
*arranged for 2 mandolins
by John Holenko*

Menuet in G
from *The Anna Magdalena Notebook*

J. S. Bach
*arranged for 2 mandolins
by John Holenko*

Musette

from *The Anna Magdalena Notebook*

J. S. Bach
*arranged for 2 mandolins
by John Holenko*

54

Musette

J. S. Bach
*arranged for 2 mandolins
by John Holenko*

Prelude No. 5
from *The Well-Tempered Clavier*

J. S. Bach
*arranged for 2 mandolins
by John Holenko*

Prelude in D minor

J. S. Bach
*arranged for 2 mandolins
by John Holenko*

♩=108

61

Prelude in F
from *the Little Clavier Book for W.F. Bach*

J. S. Bach
*arranged for 2 mandolins
by John Holenko*

Preludio

J. S. Bach
*arranged for 2 mandolins
by John Holenko*

Rondeau
from *Partita No. 2*

J. S. Bach
*arranged for 2 mandolins
by John Holenko*

Sarabande
from *Partita No. 2*

J. S. Bach
*arranged for 2 mandolins
by John Holenko*

70

Polonaise
from *The Anna Magdalena Notebook*

J. S. Bach
*arranged for 2 mandolins
by John Holenko*